THE LITTLE BOOK OF YORKSHIRE CUSTOMS & FOLKLORE

compiled by
Julia Smith

Dalesman

First published in Great Britain 2012 by Dalesman Publishing
an imprint of
Country Publications Ltd
The Water Mill, Broughton Hall
Skipton, North Yorkshire BD23 3AG

Text © Julia Smith 2012
Illustrations © Peter Kearney 2012

ISBN 978-1-85568-308-2

All rights reserved. This book must not be circulated in any form of binding or cover other than that in which it is published and without similar condition of this being imposed on the subsequent purchaser. No part of this publication may be reproduced, stored on a retrieval system or transmitted in any form, or by any means, electronic, mechanical, photocopying, recording or otherwise, without either prior permission in writing from the publisher or a licence permitting restricted copying. In the United Kingdom such licences are issued by the Copyright Licensing Agency, 90 Tottenham Court Road, London WIP 9HE. The right of Julia Smith to be identified as author of this work has been asserted in accordance with Copyright, Designs and Patents Acts 1988.

Printed in Singapore by Tien Wah Press.

Introduction

I had no trouble in finding material to include in this compilation, as Yorkshire is a veritable hotspot of old and new wonderful and sometimes weird customs, while folk-tales and legends abound in the wild and lonely corners of the county. I hope this little book will encourage locals and visitors to seek them out.

Julia Smith

All in, a bottle of gin,
All out, a bottle of stout

rhyme for running in or out
at Scarborough skipping

Lincoln was,
and London is,
and York shall be
the fairest city of the three

proverb

The Denby Dale Pie of 1815
contained mutton, fowl and
sixty-three small birds but fell to
the ground when the table broke.
The 15,000-strong crowd scrambled
on the ground and ate the pieces —
even though it had been condemned.

Housewives made Wilfra tarts for St Wilfrid's feast in Ripon and left them on the doorstep for passers-by to help themselves.

John Wainhouse of Halifax was so angry at Sir Henry Edwards' success in growing Yorkshire's first pineapple that he extended his dye-works chimney until it overlooked Edwards' property. Wainhouse topped his 270-foot (80 m) tower with a fancy cupola.

Mary Frith was a sixteenth-century highwaywoman who dressed as man and, armed with sword and pistol, rode out to rob travellers. Her success earned her the nickname of Mall Cut-Purse.

A farmer, wanting to escape from the tricks of a resident hobthrush (another name for a hob, or a benevolent goblin) packed up and left for another farm. A passer-by remarked on this, only to hear from within a milk churn:
"Ay, we's flittin'."
On hearing this farmer said:
"If thoo's theer, we may as well gan yam ageean."

Hob Hole at Kettleness was believed to be the home of a benevolent goblin who cured children of whooping-cough, 'kink-cough' as it was known locally. Mothers took their children and chanted a rhyme asking him to "tak it off".

The Devil's Arrows, between Boroughbridge and Roecliffe.

The Devil often tried to demolish Christian churches by throwing gigantic stones at them. At Rudston he missed and the monolith stands in the churchyard. He fired four arrows at a Christian settlement at Aldborough but missed again, and three of them can still be seen, now known as the Devil's Arrows.

At Temple Newsam near Leeds beware the Blue Lady; at Newburgh Priory the White Lady; and at East Riddlesden Hall the Grey Lady — for they are all ghosts.

Anne Boynton of Burton Agnes was brutally murdered, but on her deathbed she made the family promise that her head would be kept within the house. When this was forgotten, her ghost became so aggressive that her skull was brought inside so she was able to rest in peace.

At Wentworth Castle you may be alarmed at the sight of the ghost of Thomas Wentworth wandering around with his head tucked underneath his arm.

At Nunnington in North Yorkshire, Sir Peter Loschy, together with his faithful dog, fought the Loschy Hill 'worm' (dragon) for many hours. The dragon was killed, but when the dog ran to lick the face of Sir Peter it poisoned him as it carried some of the dragon's poison.

Seventeenth-century rushbearings could become violent when two rushcarts from rival villages met, rushing at each other, trying to tilt the cart and unseat the rider so violently that injuries, even death, was not unknown. Getting drunk and having a good fight was an accepted part of the proceedings.

Rushbearing at Sowerby Bridge.

It was believed that if a barren woman embraced the phallic-shaped rushcart she would become pregnant within twelve months. A lady at Saddleworth scoffed at the tale and embraced the cart — but she bore a baby girl within a year … nor was this an isolated incident.

The prophetic streams of the East Riding, the gypseys or vipseys, were "supposed a never failing presage of famine" according to William of Newburgh in the twelfth century.

In the nineteenth century when
selling a wife at market was legal, a
husband in Hull led his wife by halter
to the market place and sold her to
their lodger for twenty guineas.
At the market cross in Bradford,
Mrs Farrar was sold to Mr Green
for just five shillings.

‘Riding the stang’ was a punishment for a man caught beating his wife. His neighbours would fasten his effigy to a ladder, carry it round the streets for three nights, shouting, blowing horns and banging drums, before finally burning it.

On Good Friday, throwl-egg was played at barrows (burial mounds) near Wold Newton. Hard-boiled eggs were throwled or rolled, the winner being the one whose egg rolled farthest. Instead of being impromptu local events, egg-rolling at Easter has become popular at many heritage sites.

On 25th September, the anniversary of the battle of Stamford Bridge, tub-shaped pies, complete with soldier, were made to commemorate the battle there in 1066, when an English soldier in a wash-tub manoeuvred under the bridge, stuck up his spear and stabbed a Viking opponent.

Gooseberries being weighed at Egton Bridge Gooseberry Show.

According to a contestant at Egton Bridge gooseberry show, the secret of producing good gooseberries was to feed them a barrelful of sheep droppings, matured and diluted to the colour of weak tea.

A mummified cat found in the wall of the medieval Church of St Thomas Becket in Heptonstall, after a storm damaged the tower in 1867, may have been walled up alive. This was not an uncommon practice as it was believed the sacrifice would protect the building. It obviously didn't!

On St Mark's E'en (24th April), a watcher in a church porch between midnight and 1am would see the spirits or forms of those who were to die during the forthcoming year pass into the church. If the watcher fell asleep, it was believed they also would die.

Here's a health to t' Marsden Cuckoo,
An' to them as walled it raand,
An' if my brothers flee away,
As sooin as t' cuckoo did that day,
It'll suit me doan to t' graand.

Market Weighton,
Robert Leighton,
A brick church
And wooden steeple,
A drunken priest
And a wicked people.

Michael Drayton describes in his seventeenth-century poem *Polyolbion* how a nymph fleeing from the clutches of a satyr is saved when she is turned into a spring. Her panting breath caused the ebb and flow of the water in the Ebbing and Flowing Well at Giggleswick.

Hilda, the Abbess of Whitby, so disliked the seagulls flying over the abbey that, through the force of her prayers, she compelled them to lower their wings and drop to the ground. The serpents she drove over the cliff turned to stone — we know them as ammonite fossils.

St Hilda's Serpents.

The legend of Semerwater relates how the village was cursed by an old man (variously a saint or angel in disguise) who was refused refreshment at every house except one, which survived when the village was swallowed by the lake, as the old man uttered this curse:

Semerwater rise,
and Semerwater sink,
And swallow the town all save this house,
Where they gave me meat and drink.

Church bells can sometimes be heard ringing beneath the waves.

A giant had also been angry at the selfishness of the villagers at Semerwater, and he hurled the Carlow Stone at them.

Beneath Stone Raise, a large cairn overlooking Semerwater, lies a chest of gold dropped by a giant on his way to Pendragon Castle. One day a fairy will reveal this treasure to a mortal who will then be able to remove it easily, providing he doesn't speak or swear.

The devil is said to have leapt from Scar Top at Netherton to Castle Hill at Almondbury, a distance of eight miles (13 km). Once there, he wandered around the five passages that supposedly exist underground. Another legend tells of a buried golden cradle, with or without a dragon guardian.

At Willy Howe, a barrow (burial mound) in North Yorkshire, a drunken traveller was offered a drink from a cup at a fairy banquet here. However, he had sense enough not to drink from it and be captured; he threw away the drink and made off with the cup.

Willy Howe was also where a chest of gold was discovered. The finders attached a train of horses to it but, however hard they heaved, the deeper it sank — and was never recovered. Perhaps they were up against the fairies who lived there?

Wishing stones are to be found all around the country, and Brimham Rocks had its own. It was traditional to place the middle finger of one's right hand in the hole in the stone and make a wish.

Find the wishing stone at Brimham Rocks to make a wish.

In a rock-hewn chamber deep below Richmond Castle, King Arthur and his Knights sleep until England is in dire peril, when they will arise from their slumbers to go forth and save the country. With them hang an enchanted sword and an enchanted horn.

According to legend, beneath Guisborough Priory lies a secret tunnel and halfway along lies a chest of gold guarded by a raven. When a brave soul stole down and confronted the raven, it suddenly turned into the Devil.

The Dragon of Wantley came down to terrorise the people from a cave amongst Wharncliffe Crags, near Sheffield, known as the Dragon's Den. The legend incorporates sacred or mystic numbers, the beast having seven heads, twice seven eyes and eating up to three children a night.

The name of a round barrow in North Yorkshire, Drake Howe, may derive from Dragon Howe as it was believed to contain treasure guarded by a dragon.

Servants walking home from Benjamin Ferrand's house, St Ives in Harden near Bingley, saw him ride up to the entrance gates and so they rushed to open them for him. They later discovered that he had died that same night before he reached home.

At the village feast, a wooden image of St Peter, the patron saint of Nun Monkton, used to be buried with due ceremony on Maypole Hill. On the little feast day (the day before the feast) a procession of villagers, led by a fiddler, disinterred him and brought him back.

"At Halifax
the law so sharp doth deal
That whoso more
than thirteen pence doth steal
They have a gyn*
that wondrous quick and well
Sends thieves all headless
to heaven or hell."

**gibbet*

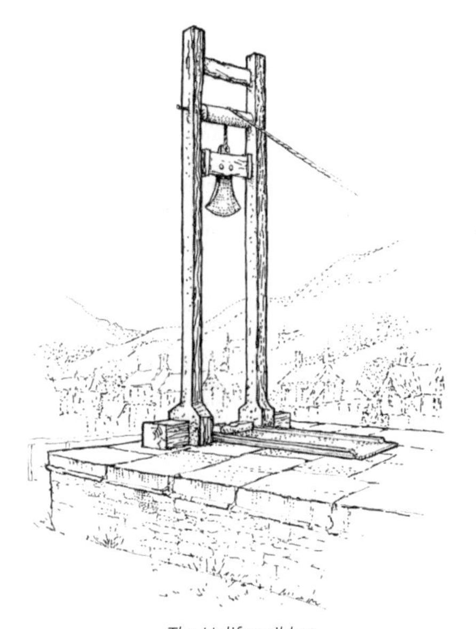

The Halifax gibbet.

Many churches around the country have traditions relating how, during their construction, the stones were constantly removed during the night — and Yorkshire has five churches like this. At Holme-on-the-Wolds, fairies were responsible for moving the stones to a new site.

A man walked past Elbolton Hill near Grassington one evening and saw a group of fairies dancing. He offered to sing to them, but they reacted angrily; he ran off but managed to capture a fairy and put it in his pocket. When he reached home, the fairy had flown.

A witch sold her soul to the Devil but then refused to give it up and flew off with the Devil in pursuit. Unable to catch her, he flung a handful of earth at her, making the Hole at Horcum. He missed, dropped it — and that became Blakey Topping.

An alternative legend relates that when Wade was building a causeway so his wife, Bell, could walk over the moor to milk her cow, he took handfuls of earth, leaving the Hole of Horcum; any leftover earth he pushed aside, creating Blakey Topping.

Beware meeting a phantom hound, known in Yorkshire as the Barguest, as this is an omen of death. You might encounter this great black dog with the huge saucer-shaped eyes in Egton and other parts of the county, but you are safe if you cross water.

It was the custom to throw bent
pins into St John's Well at Mount
Grace Priory, then fervently to
make a wish in the silence of
your heart for it to be fulfilled.

Tales of secret burials were tested when the ruins of the Lady Chapel at Mount Grace Priory were excavated. It appeared they were true, as human bones were found pushed aside to allow a grand burial with an oak coffin made after the chapel fell into disuse and ruin.

The last Sunday in Lent was known in the West Riding as 'Spanish' Sunday. Spanish (liquorice) was soaked in a bottle overnight, then filled with water from a local holy well or spring. A good shake and it was ready to drink.

Tid, Mid, Miseray, Carlin, Paum and Paste-egg Day were the medieval names for the Sundays in Lent.

"For feeals an' thick heads,
cum ti Pathrington*"

**Patrington*

The Bingley Bletherheads was
an annual carnival at which playing
the fool was the main attraction.
A blether is dialect for bladder, so a
bletherhead was a man with a skull
like a bladder, ie empty.

A chair that once stood in the Busby Stoop Inn near Thirsk was where the ghost of Thomas Busby liked to rest. He was hanged, where the inn now stands, for the murder of his father-in-law, and anyone sitting in his chair suffered a fatal accident soon afterwards.

In pagan times, rivers, like wells,
were believed to be under the
protection of a goddess or spirit.
The River Wharfe was associated
with the goddess or spirit Verbeia
who possessed life-giving and
life-taking powers.

"The shelving slimy River Don,
Each year a daughter or a son"

Another example of a river claiming lives

Many standing stones were believed to turn round, daily, nightly or on one day in the year, when they heard the cock crow. Stump John is a cock-crow stone at Hollow Meadows near Sheffield.

Prehistoric standing stones at Barnby and near Goldsborough take their name from the giant Wade. Another stone (now missing), eleven feet (3 m) away from the Barnby one, supposedly marked the head and foot of his grave.

St Blaize became the patron saint of woolcombers as he was scraped to death by iron combs. In Bradford a procession of all involved in the woollen industry was held every seven years. Over 800 people took part in 1825 when the industry was at its height.

St Lawrence had such a bad name in the Bingley area of West Yorkshire that it was said of an idle person: "I see Leng Lawrence has gotten howd on tha".

The Boar's Well and and the Spink Well in Bradford were associated with a legendary wild boar that had been terrorising the city. When a hunter came on it as it drank, he killed it with his spear and cut out its tongue to claim the reward offered for its death.

The superstitious leadminers of Greenhow in Nidderdale believed they should never go below alone, as the trolls who resided there would attack a lone man, but there was safety in numbers. A miner determined to go alone was later found dead with strange marks around his throat.

The first person to enter the house at Christmas and New Year in the North Riding must be a dark-haired male; in other areas a fair-haired person is considered lucky. In most places a red-haired person was considered unlucky.

Around twelve tons of gingerbread were sold annually at Whitby at one time, as gingerbread, together with cheese, was a large part of the Christmas fare. Gingerbread and cheese were also part of the lying-in fare after the birth of a child.

The village of Sessay near Thirsk was terrorised by a one-eyed ogre, until Sir Guy Dawnay killed him by stabbing the monster through his eye after the ogre had been knocked to the ground by one of the sails on the windmill. Sir Guy could then claim the hand of a local heiress.

In the seventeenth century, William Willance presented a chalice to Ripon corporation in thanks for escaping with his life when he and his horse fell over the edge of Whitcliffe Scar one night in thick fog. (His horse was not so lucky.)

Boatmen who lived and worked on their narrow boats liked to decorate them, and there were a number of ways this could be done. The boatmen on the Leeds-Liverpool Canal favoured Victorian scrollwork.

Narrow boat on a Yorkshire canal.

Stealing maypoles was an age-old tradition which also took away the 'luck', or fertility, associated with it, leaving women and cattle barren, and crops unfertilised. Maypoles were banned by the Puritan parliament but reinstated when Charles II came to the throne.

Behind a pub in the village of Asenby, between Thirsk and Ripon, is turf labyrinth. Another one nearby was maintained by one family in the traditional way. Unlike a maze, a labyrinth has no misleading turns.

When the giant Rombald was fleeing from his stone-throwing wife, he slipped, leaving the imprint of his foot on the rock known as the Cow, on Ilkley Moor, while his heel knocked down the small rock known as the Calf.

Legendary cows providing a constant supply of milk for all-comers and also producing a calf appear in different parts of the country, but one folk-tale relates how the cow and calf, after being treated badly, turned to stone — which might apply to the Cow and Calf on Ilkley Moor.

Many people once again like to watch the sunrise on the summer solstice, 21st June, at stone circles. The Twelve Apostles on Ilkley Moor has become a popular site for those wishing to become more attuned to the landscape.

A goose is believed to have landed on
Gormire Lake, sailed into a gully
beneath Whitestone Cliff and later
appeared, shorn of its feathers,
some twelve miles (19 km) away
at Kirkbymoorside.

On Christmas Day and New Year's Day it was considered unlucky to throw anything out of the house, not even the ashes from the fire or the dust swept from the house.

Vessel cups were small boxes
containing a cheap wax doll
representing the baby Jesus
surrounded by greenery or fruit.
These were taken from house to
house in the Christmas season by
poor, single females who sang
God Rest Ye Merry Gentlemen in return
for a few coins.

We all eat pancakes on Shrove Tuesday, but what about collops on the day before, hash (Ash) Wednesday; fritter or frutter Thursday — in Cleveland it was bloody (ie black pudding) Thursday; and fish Friday?

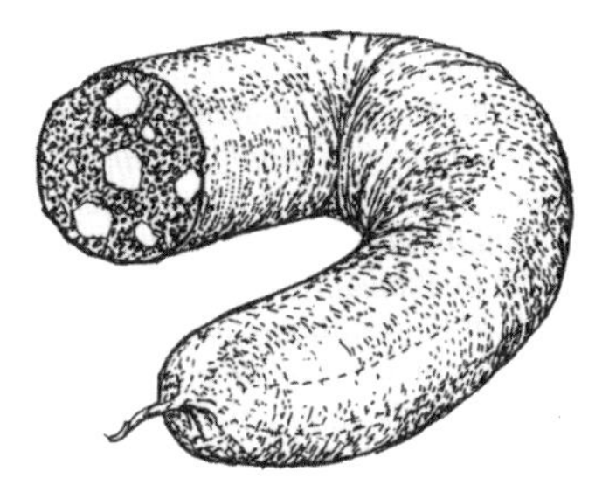

Black pudding.

Margaret Wharton was a rich maiden lady who earned herself the nickname of Peg Pennyworth because of her habit of buying only small quantities of goods, including a pennyworth of live eels she carried home in her pocket.

When a man was driving his horse
and cart past the home of Old
Nanny Rowley of Weaverthorpe, his
horse stopped and refused to move.
Believing she had bewitched it, he
rushed inside and struck her cheek
and, as the blood began to flow,
her powers ceased.

The Wise Woman of Littondale was a familiar figure in Kettlewell and the surrounding area. So afraid of her were some young people that they would leap over the nearest wall at her approach. She was renowned for her incantations and divinations.

After Christopher Pivett's house in York burnt down, he slept fully clothed downstairs (but not in a bed in case the house burnt down again) for forty years prior to his death in 1796. He was buried with the skull he always kept by him.

William Batt, the master of Oakwell Hall, was seen going up the stairs of his home, on which he left a bloody footstep, at the exact time of his murder in London in 1684.

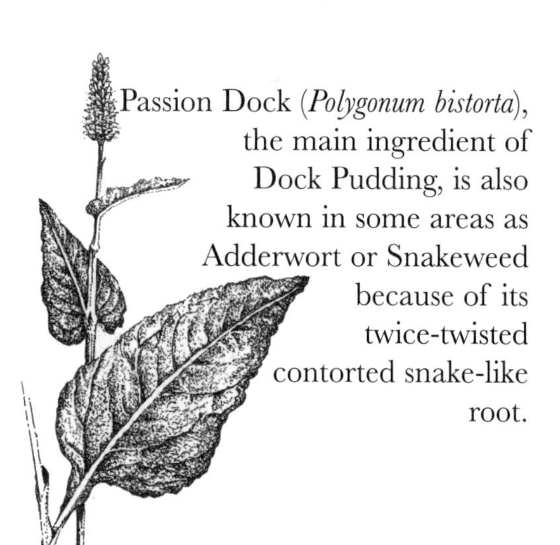

Passion Dock (*Polygonum bistorta*), the main ingredient of Dock Pudding, is also known in some areas as Adderwort or Snakeweed because of its twice-twisted contorted snake-like root.

At the Hubberholme 'Parliament', on the first Monday in January, farmers bid for sixteen acres (6.5 ha) of pasture during the time it takes for a candle, lit at the beginning of the auction, to burn down. The proceeds benefit the poor and the sick.

The fairies used Claymore Well near Kettleness, on the Yorkshire coast, to wash, bleach and beat their clothes; the sound of the latter could be heard as far away as Runswick Bay.

Janet's (or Jennet's) Foss, near Malham, conceals the cave of Janet, Queen of the Fairies. The waterfall is also a place for water sprites who like such places in order to fiddle to the accompaniment of falling water.

Fairy Cross Plain lies between the remote dells of Great and Little Fryup in the North York Moors. 'Fry' derives from the Norse goddess Freya who is sometimes associated with the fairy and spirit realms. (This may explain why fairies have been seen playing here.)

Possibly the most famous fairies are those photographed playing by a stream in Cottingley. Though most of the photographs were faked, one of the girls who saw them always claimed that the final photo of the fairies was not.

It was customary at the funeral of an
unmarried woman to carry before
the corpse a white garland with a
glove in the centre bearing the name
and (a bit cruel, this!) her age.
The garland was later suspended
from the roof of the church.

Corpse ways were so named as they were used to transport corpses from remote communities to church for burial. Some of these routes are now used as footpaths, the most famous being the Lyke Wake Walk with its accompanying dirge.

If the shirt or shift dress of a sick person was thrown into a well in Cliffrigg Wood near Great Ayton and floated, the person would recover; if it sank, they wouldn't. Rags were hung on the bushes around the well as an offering to its patron St Oswald.

In order to dream of their future husbands, three young women would make and share a Dumb Cake. Each ate a bit of her share, wrapped the rest in a stocking from her left leg and put it under her pillow after she had silently walked backwards to bed.

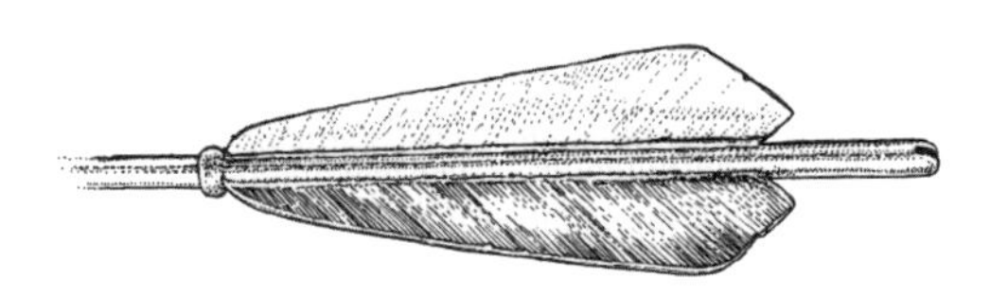

The Society of Archers, founded by archers in the North Riding and South Durham, held their first tournament to shoot for an 'Antient Silver Arrow' at Scorton in 1673 — and the tournament is still going strong, making it the oldest recorded sporting event in the world.

Runners wearing nothing but shoes
would once race up and down the
hills and fells of the Dales and
Pennines. If a runner could not clear
a wall with a single leap, he was
unlikely to win the race for fairly
obvious reasons.

In 1766, a young woman was driven to suicide because of being ill-treated by her lover. She threw herself from Almscliffe Crags, but a strong wind inflated her clothes, which then acted as a parachute causing her to float gracefully to the ground below. (The young woman may have glimpsed the fairies on her way down as they have a parlour among the rocks.)

The last remaining sheaf of corn left in the field after cutting was said to embody the corn spirit and, in order not to be the reaper solely responsible for killing her, the reapers, standing in a semi-circle, took turns to throw their sickles at it.

Corn dolly made from the last sheaf of corn to be cut.

There are many caves in the cliffs at Flamborough; onc of them, Robin Lythe's Hole, has a fifty-foot (15 m) high roof, and is named after a local smuggler.

Boundary riding at Richmond originated from royal charters of 1576 and 1668; in order to impress the exact location of the boundary on them, young people were bumped on the ground or were bent over stones and beaten.

"Carlin Sunday we kep up
Wi grey pez cooked fer t'supper;
They're steeped in watter ower neet,
Then fried wi saim [lard] or butter."

Carling Sunday is the fifth Sunday in Lent, when folk in the East Riding ate these peas.

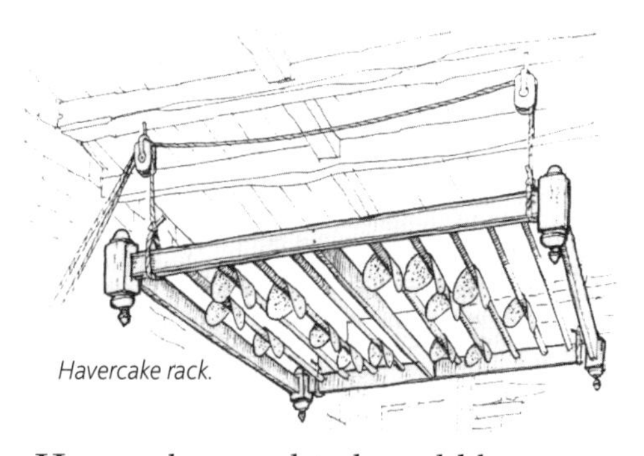

Havercake rack.

Havercakes used to be sold by a man wearing a white apron and pushing a handcart to housewives in the early twentieth century. A type of cake, havercakes were sold fresh, then hung on a bread rack to become dry and crisp over the kitchen fire.

To avoid Os's death by drowning on
a particular day as predicted, his
mother took him up Roseberry
Topping, away from water.
Unfortunately he wandered off,
fell in a well and was drowned
while she slept. When she died soon
after, she was buried beside him
— in Os-mother-ley.

The clay soil of Cleveland
is recalled in the saying:

"Cleveland in the clay,
bring two shoes
and carry one away."

The Hand of Glory was a hand taken from a criminal hanging on the gallows, pickled and then a lighted candle, made from the fat of another such hand, was placed in it. The Hand of Glory had the power to put people into a profound sleep, making it a great help to burglars.

Hepworth Feast originated to commemorate the village's deliverance from the Great Plague of 1665. To prevent the spread of the disease, the infected area was sealed off and anyone trying to cross it was threatened with death. (Of course if they were infected they would die anyway.)

The reluctance of the Ripon mayor-elect to take office is recalled at the annual mayor-making, where a search for him takes place. This refers to the refusal of some to take the office of wakeman, who was responsible for the safety of the town during the night. His duties began at 9pm when the horn was blown, and lasted until dawn.

The Wakeman's Horn, blown every night in Ripon.

Childermas (28th December) was considered extremely unlucky. On this day a member of the crew of a fishing vessel, persuaded by his wife, refused to sail. The voyage was successful but, when the fisherman next sailed, the boat was lost with all hands.

When most of the men living
at Runswick were fishermen,
their children playing on the
cliffs would chant:

"Souther, wind, souther,
And blow father home to mother."

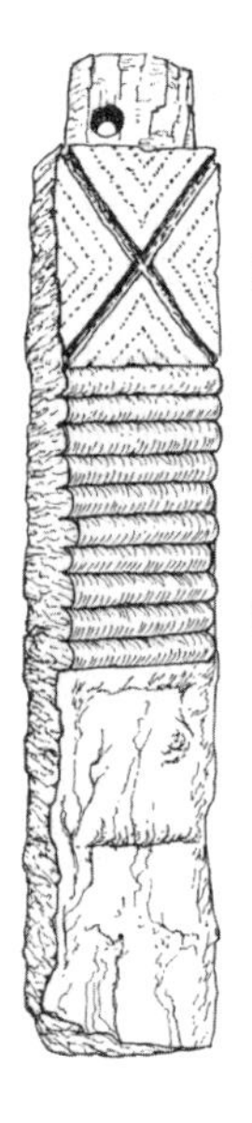

Many houses in and around the North York Moors were protected from witches by witch posts. Made of wood and carved at the top, they were built into the structure of the house.

An imp known as Red Cap often helped a farmer at Draughton near Skipton during hay time. He was rewarded with a cup of milk or, in stormy weather, a place by the fireside. If in an ill-humour, Red Cap would resort to playing evil pranks on the farmer.

"Shake a bridle over the gravc of a Yorkshireman and he will rise and steal a horse."

proverb

The excellence of the spurs made
in Ripon led to the saying
'As true steel as Ripon rowels'.

Fugitives who sought sanctuary in Beverley Minster in the fifteenth and sixteenth centuries included two female murderers, over two hundred debtors, and seven coiners. Daggers, lances, spears, a sword and two pitchforks were used as murder weapons. Anyone seeking sanctuary could do so by sitting in the frith stool, a stone chair next to the altar.

The sanctuary chair in Beverley Minster.

An old East Riding remedy to clear the face of spots or freckles was to smear with the blood of a white hen, leave to dry, then wipe away.

A swollen throat could be eased
by a plaster of burnt swallows
and their nests.

A hellfire club was held at Skelton Castle in the eighteenth century, earning it the nickname 'the crazy castle'.

Some of the reasons given to me for keeping our Yorkshire customs and folklore alive include:

"Without tradition and custom, the community would fall apart."

"It's part of our heritage."

"It's a focus for the community."

"Because we've always done it."

Other books published by Dalesman:

The Little Book of Yorkshire
The Little Book of Yorkshire Humour
The Little Book of Yorkshire Dialect
The Little Book of Yorkshire Christmas
The Little Book of Dickie Bird
The Little Book of Lancashire
The Little Book of the Lake District
The Little Book of Country Sayings

For a full list of our books, calendars,
DVDs, videos and magazines,
visit www.dalesman.co.uk.